Reuben C. Lawrence, Jr.

GOD'S WORD

As I See It In My Mind

A Bible Study for Young Adults

God the Son

God the Father

God the Holy Spirit

GOD'S WORD

As I See It In My Mind

A Bible Study for Young Adults

by
Reuben C. Lawrence, Jr.

LOWBAR
PUBLISHING COMPANY

905 South Douglas Avenue • Nashville, Tennessee 37204
Phone: 615-972-2842
E-mail: Lowbarpublishingcompany@gmail.com
Web site: www.Lowbarbookstore.com

GOD'S WORD: AS I SEE IT IN MY MIND
Copyright © 2010: Reuben C. Lawrence, Jr.
Printed 2014

Editor: Lalita Smith
Graphic and Cover Design Artist: Norah S. Branch

ISBN: 978-0-9886237-9-8

Lowbar Publishing Company
Nashville, Tennessee 37204
615-972-2842
E-mail: Lowbarpublishingcompany@gmail.com
Website: www.Lowbarbookstore.com

For additional information and to contact the author for workshops or seminars:

Reuben C. Lawrence, Jr.
825 W. Nocturne Drive
Nashville, Tennessee 37207
615-881-2403
E-mail: rcljr510@gmail.com

Scripture references in this book are taken from the King James Version of the Holy Bible, unless otherwise noted.

All rights reserved under the International Copyright Law.

Contents and/or cover may not be reproduced in whole or in part in any form without the expressed written consent of the author or publisher.

*Dedicated to the Memory
of
My Loving Wife
DeBarbara Lawrence*

December 14, 1953—December 20, 2008

TABLE OF CONTENTS

Page

Preface viii

Introduction 1

Opening Praise: Matthew 7:7-8
Lesson No. 1: JESUS WALKS ON WATER 3

Opening Praise: John 1:1-5
Lesson No. 2: THE TEN LEPERS 12

Opening Praise: Psalm 100
Lesson No. 3: LEAP OF FAITH/ THE WAY
 WE USE TO HAVE CHURCH 22

Opening Praise: Psalm 107:1-7
Lesson No. 4: 2 CHRONICLES 7:14 32

Opening Praise: John 15:15-17
Lesson No. 5: 1 PETER 2:9-10 38

References 46

About the Author 47

Preface

The vision and concept for these lessons comes from my personal relationship with God, and a burning desire to educate His people.

GOD'S WORD: "AS I SEE IT IN MY MIND," is my personal perception of Scripture. It is the way I understand His Word. The things, I have been able to see, comes from combining the use of my mind with the "insight" of the Spirit of Truth working together through my imagination. I thank God for the anointing and gift of teaching the saints of God. I asked God to expand my territory of thinking, so that I, and others can see His Word from a massive, but interesting mindset.

My view of God has been limited to understanding God as preachers and teachers, and even as I, myself have presented Him to others. But now, I envision God on a greater plane. He has given us the road map to all of life's situations, and the solutions to them as well.

My hope and prayer is that these teachings will be visionary and edifying, unorthodox yet informative, profound but understanding, to all who reads or hears them.

This series of sermons has been on my heart for some time, but I have struggled within myself because of my inability to trust God completely for the success of this ministry.

Finally, my brothers and sisters in Christ, I realize that I can only teach you after the Spirit has taught me first. So I say to my soul; be encouraged, *"For God has not given us a spirit of fear, but of power and of love and of a sound mind"* (II Timothy 1:7).

Introduction

This first compilation of sermons which can be used as Bible Studies comes from the many hours I have spent in study of the Holy Scriptures. It is my desire to make Bible study enjoyable for you as a youth, young adult, or mature reader. This is important because Paul urges all who are in Christ to, "*Study to shew thyself approved unto God, a workman that needeth not to be ashamed, rightly dividing the word of truth*" (2 Tim. 2:15, KJV). I believe this applies even more so for those called to teach.

What exactly does "Rightly divide" mean? It is the Greek term *orthotomeo*; which is a compound of *orthos*, meaning straight, upright, not crooked; and *tomos*, which speaks of cutting incisively. Basically, it means we are to "teach correctly, formally, and guide on a straight path." Thus, if you are to be trained by the Word of God, you must have it presented in such a way, so that you will not only study it, but practice what you study.

HOW TO USE THIS BOOK AS A STUDY GUIDE

For clarity, sermons are referred to as lessons. These first five lessons are designed for use with young adults ages thirteen and up. For preachers, these lessons can be used as scriptural nuggets for the development of a myriad of prophetic messages. They will help you as a teacher to walk through the Scriptures verse-by-verse and expound upon key words, events, messages, actions of Jesus Christ and the disciples, and explore hidden insights and revelations.

For the young person who wishes to study alone, it is plainly written so that you can open your Bible, read, and follow each lesson, one verse at a time. I have added a "Life Application" section at the end of each lesson. It is important, especially in today's world, to know how to make the truths of God's word applicable to your life today.

Lastly, you will find several questions at the end of each lesson for use if hosting a group study format, or during individual study times. It is important to answer these questions, as by doing so, you will fix the lesson in your memory and retain further the wisdom gleaned from your time of study. Where there is a verse of scripture to commit to memory, please take the time to do this. The Psalmist David admonishes us all saying, *"Thy word have I hid in mine heart, that I might not sin against thee"* (Psalm 119:11).

Opening Praise

Matthew 7:7-8

"Ask, and it shall be given to you; seek and you will find; knock, and it will be opened to you. For everyone who asks receives, and he who seeks finds, and to him who knocks it will be opened."

Lesson No. 1 — JESUS WALKS ON WATER

Matthew 14:22-33
Mark 6: 45-51
John 6: 15-21
Matthew 14:22

Before the miracles recorded in this lesson, Jesus walks on water. Notice that I said miracles, with an "s." Jesus had just finished feeding 5,000 men besides women and children, and the twelve disciples. There were twelve baskets left over.

"AS I SEE IT IN MY MIND," there were twelve baskets left over, one for each one of the disciples. After the miracle, John 6:15 records that, *"When Jesus perceived that they were about to come and take him by force to make him king, he departed again to the mountain to pray."* Matthew adds the fact that immediately, Jesus made his disciples get into the boat to go before him to the other side. Remember the word "_immediately_" because we will see it again. Jesus had every intention of joining the disciples, because the scripture says, they were to go before him, *"To the other side."*

Matthew 14:23

After sending the multitudes home, Jesus departs to the mountain, alone, to pray. Jesus did this often, keeping his relationship with his Father intact. Even at Jesus' baptism, He was praying when the Holy Spirit descended upon Him. For additional study on this subject, refer to Luke 3:21, 22.

Matthew 14:24

The boat was in the midst of the sea, about three miles out. The Sea of Galilee (or Tiberius) was six miles across. Now the boat was being tossed to and fro by the waves, and the wind, which was contrary, in opposition, or against them. The wind usually aided them to their destination, but here it was hindering their progress. They were in a storm.

Matthew 14:25

Jesus standing on land, during the fourth watch of the night, between 3:00 a.m. through 6:00 a.m. Mark 6:48 records that Jesus saw, (*perceived*), his disciples straining at rowing. The Greek word for saw here is *"eidon"* – not the act of seeing with the eyes, but the actual perception of the object. *(Dakes's Annotated Reference Bible).* Jesus had the conscious knowing (*awareness*) that his disciples were in trouble, and in need of help.

"AS I SEE IT IN MY MIND," this is the first miracle that occurred that night. Think about it, Jesus was able to see (*perceive*) his disciples, between 3:00 a.m. and 6:00 a.m. in the morning, in the pitch black dark of night, in a storm, in the midst of the sea, three miles away, tossed to and fro, trying to stay alive. So, what did He do? Jesus went to them, walking on the sea.

Mark 6:48 also says that, *"He would have passed by them."* He is actually coming (*or going*) to their rescue. Here is Jesus, walking on water, in the midst of a storm, the boat being tossed to and fro, the wind was against them, but none of the forces of nature have an effect on Jesus. Of note is the fact that the storm, (*the waves and the wind*), had not impeded the progress of Jesus, but the storm does have the boat and the disciples struggling in the middle of the sea. Again, Mark 6:48 says Jesus would have passed by them, proving that Jesus was walking faster than the boat was moving.

"AS I SEE IT IN MY MIND," this is the second miracle of the night and reminds me of the words of a song which are::

"Like a ship that's tossed and drive; battered by an angry sea, when the storms of life are raging, and their fury falls on me. I wonder what I have done, that makes this race so hard to run; then I say to my soul, don't worry, Oh, the Lord will make a way somehow." —*T. A. Dorsey*

This is the miracle that we all see so plainly, the story is based on this written account; Jesus walks on water, the third miracle.

Matthew 14:26

"When the disciples saw Jesus walking on the sea, they were troubled, frightened, and afraid. They thought it was a ghost, and cried out for fear."

This is a natural reaction for humans when we don't recognize something; it scares us. As if the disciples didn't have enough trouble, fighting for their lives, the boat being tossed to and fro, the wind against them, they weren't making any progress, they were straining at rowing, now they see a man, (Jesus), walking on the sea.

Matthew 14:27

But "immediately" Jesus speaks to them, "Be of good cheer, it is I, do not be afraid."

Jesus at once identifies himself so the disciples would know that help isn't on the way, it is here; it has arrived: Jesus to the rescue. "AS I SEE IT IN MY MIND," Jesus lets them know that he is right in the midst of the storm with them. When your ship is being tossed to and fro, the waves of life have you in a struggle, and the winds of trouble are blowing against everything you are trying to do, and you are fighting to survive, here comes Jesus, just when you need Him to help get you out of the storm.

Matthew 14:28

Now Peter, it doesn't surprise me, answers Jesus, and asks a question. Peter says, "*Lord, if it is you, command me to come to you on the water.*" Peter reminds me of myself in a lot of ways. He was bold, a fighter, hard, outspoken, a coward at times, and known to curse and swear. Peter of all people, knew exactly who Jesus was. Later, in Matthew 16:13-18, Jesus asked his disciples "*Who do men say that I am?*"

They answered, "*Some say John the Baptist, some Elijah, some Jeremiah, or one of the prophets.*" Jesus asked, "*But who do you say that I am?*"

Peter said "*Thou are the Christ, the Son of the Living God.*" I believe because of the waves and the wind, together with their battle to survive the storm, Peter doubted that it was Jesus. Why? I suppose that his mind and energy is focused on the surrounding events and activities at hand. "AS I SEE IT IN MY MIND," Peter did not doubt Jesus, but himself. How much can I trust my faith, and believe that Jesus is who he says *that he is?*

Matthew 14:29

Jesus tells Peter, "*Come!*"

The scripture says that when Peter got out of the boat, he walked on the water to go to Jesus. Peter also exhibits power over nature under the power and protection of Jesus' word. Although the waves are still raging, the wind was against them, the boat was tossed to and fro, but the storm likewise had no effect on Peter, because he was under the power and protection of Jesus. This was the fourth miracle.

Matthew 14:30

As long as Peter kept his eyes on Jesus, he walked on water, but when Peter took his eyes off Jesus, and looked at or (*saw*) the events going on around him, things changed. Looking at circumstances instead of Jesus caused Peter to lose faith. Peter saw, (*perceived*) that the wind was boisterous, and he became afraid. Peter couldn't actually see the wind, he felt the wind, and saw the effects of it. When the storms of life are raging, and in the midst of the winds of disappointment, sorrow, sickness, or financial woes, keep looking to Jesus for help. Focus on Him, and Him only, not friends or loved ones.

We, like Peter, will sink every time we take our eyes off Jesus and look at the difficulties of the situation we face. Psalm 46:1 reads, "*God is our refuge and strength, a very present help in trouble."* Peter's plight is caused by his lack of faith and trust in Jesus. He became distracted by his surroundings, and lost focus on who was in control, and who was causing these two miracles to happen. Let's not let our minds wander away from Jesus, who takes care of us in all situations. Peter realizes that he is sinking, and cried out for Jesus to save him. We cry out in despair, just like Peter did when we began to sink, especially when it's our own doing.

Matthew 14:31

And "immediately," at this instance, at once, Jesus stretched forth his hand and caught him, and asked him, O you of little faith, why did you doubt? "

"AS I SEE IT IN MY MIND," Jesus is saying, Peter, you asked to come out here, and I have given you power to withstand the wind and the waves, the storm has no effect on you. I have given you what you asked for, to walk on water, so why didn't you trust me and keep the faith? My friend, look to Jesus, who is the author and finisher of your faith. Jesus saves His children even if we are not looking. Now this has happened to me. I was driving and my cell phone rang and I was distracted enough to have wrecked. I've learned that Jesus saves you when you aren't even looking.

Remember, that Jesus and Peter are still in a storm, in the midst of the sea, the disciples still straining at rowing; the boat is tossed to and fro by the wind, but they are still in the storm together. Jesus won't abandon you in the midst of your storm, no matter how severe it may become. This was the fifth miracle. Can you imagine Jesus standing on water, and holding up Peter also?

Matthew 14:32

"And when they (Jesus and Peter), got into the boat, the wind ceased."

Finally, the disciples and the boat are out of the storm. "AS I SEE IT IN MY MIND," Jesus has the full measure of the Holy Spirit. He has power over nature, performed supernatural miracles, and also has power over all creation. He should have because according to John 1: 1-3, *"In the beginning was the Word, and the Word was with God, and the Word was God. He was in the beginning with God. All things were made by Him, and without Him was not anything made that was made."*

Jesus knows when we are in a storm. He knows when we are overpowered by the waves of trouble on every side, blown in all directions by the winds of life, making no progress, tossed to and fro by this problem or that problem. Jesus always comes to the rescue and is not affected by the troubles of this world or the forces of nature. Once Jesus got on board, everything was back to normal. He calms the storms of life even when we don't look exclusively at Him for help. This was the sixth miracle.

Matthew 14:33

Then, after all of the miraculous events that had just occurred, everyone in the boat worshipped Jesus. Of course they were thankful that they didn't perish in the storm, and because Jesus had come to their rescue. Now, all recognized Him as the *"Son of God."*

AS I SEE IT IN MY MIND," John 6:21 says, "Then they willingly received him into the ship: and immediately the ship was at the land whither they went." (KJV) They were on the Sea of Galilee, or the Sea of Tiberius, which was six miles wide. They were instantly at the other side of the Sea, at their destination. We always get where we are going when Jesus gets on board. This was the 7th miracle.

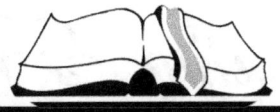

LIFE APPLICATION

Describe in detail the storm you last faced or, are currently facing.
_____
_____
_____
_____
_____

What did you glean from this lesson that will help you today or in the future?
_____
_____
_____

REVIEW / DISCUSSION QUESTIONS

1. Why is fear something most people struggle with? _____
   _____
   _____

2. Even after Jesus has spoken His word, have you lacked the courage to obey? _____

3. After seeing Peter walk on the water, who do you think the next disciple would have been to ask Jesus to do the same? And why? _____
   _____
   _____
   _____

Opening Praise

JOHN 1:1-5

*In the beginning was the Word,
And the Word was with God, and the Word was God.
The same was in the beginning with God.
All things were made through Him,
And without Him nothing was made that was made.
In Him was life, and the life was the light of men.
And the light shines in the darkness,
And the darkness did not comprehend it.*

Lesson No. 2 — JESUS HEALS TEN LEPERS

Luke 17:11-19

This is a very complex lesson because it covers so many topics that need to be taught to God's people. I will expound on each of the following:

    A. Courage and Hope

    B. Positioning

    C. Faith

    D. Obedience

    E. Thankfulness

    F. Opportunity to all

    G. Salvation

To set a chronological timeline for the text, let's look at Luke 13:31-33, which says: "On that very day some of the Pharisees came, saying to him, *"Get out and depart from here, for Herod wants to kill you!"* And He said to them, *"Go, tell that fox, Behold,*

I cast out demons and perform cures today and tomorrow, and the third day I shall be perfected. Nonetheless I must journey today, tomorrow, and the day following; for it cannot be that a prophet should perish outside of Jerusalem." Then John 11: 53-57 adds, *"Then, from that day on, they plotted to put Him to death. Therefore Jesus no longer walked openly among the Jews, but went from there into the country near the wilderness, to a city called Ephraim, and there remained with his disciples. And the Jew's Passover was near, and many went from the country up to Jerusalem before the Passover, to purify themselves. Then they sought Jesus, and spoke among themselves as they stood in the temple; what do you think--that He will not come to the feast? Now both the chief priests and the Pharisees had given a command, that if anyone knew where He was, he should report it, that they might seize Him."*

Because of His teaching and miraculous healings, Herod, the Jews, the Pharisees, and the Chief Priests wanted Jesus killed. The sad part is, they were willing to do it themselves. After raising Lazarus from the dead, they not only wanted Jesus dead, but Lazarus also. Since Jesus could no longer walk openly among the Jews, the leader wondered if He would attend the Passover.

Luke 17:11

As Jesus went to Jerusalem to observe His last Passover, He passed between Samaria and Galilee, avoiding Jewish authorities, careful not to let it be known He was on His way to the feast. "AS I SEE IT IN MY MIND," Jesus is teaching me that it is not good to let everybody know where you are, or what you are planning to do, especially your enemies. Jesus isn't running from the law, but just keeping a low-profile. He was trying to avoid a confrontation with the Jews, because His time had not come.

There is an old saying that has a lot of wisdom in it: "You don't have to go to every fight you are invited to!"

Luke 17:12

"As Jesus entered a certain village, ten (10) men who were lepers, met Him, who stood afar off."

Leprosy was a serious skin disease that was very contagious, with visible sores, which sometimes covered the entire body. Leprosy was a disease in which some people were inflicted for the punishment of some particular sin. Lepers were banned by Moses law from living within the city limits. They were quarantined from people and were secluded from society. They lived separated from family, friends, loved ones, and the church. There was no known cure to man for leprosy: no medicine to alleviate the pain; the doctors couldn't help, neither could magic, or witchcraft. Only the priest could declare a leper clean or unclean. The Talmud says that lepers were to stay 100 paces or 300 feet from anyone not inflicted with the disease. If anyone unknowingly came close to a leper, they were to shout out, *"Unclean!" "Unclean!"* to warn people of their presence and closeness. Leviticus 13:46 says, *"All the days wherein the plague shall be in him he shall be defiled; he is unclean; he shall dwell alone; without the camp shall his habitation be."*

The ten lepers lived together outside the village walls, suffered from the same disease, and realized that if they had any chance of being healed, now was the moment to make a move. It is possible that they had heard about the healer and teacher called Jesus. They had hope, they exhibited courage, because they wanted healing, and they met Jesus, and got as close as they could by law.

Numbers 5:2 records this: *"Command the children of Israel that they put out of the camp every leper, and every one that hath an issue, and whosoever is defiled by the dead."* Leprosy was a disease that could affect anyone, not just sinners, as some may teach. Leprosy wasn't a rich man or a poor man's disease; it could inflict anyone. Many times we see God's wrath poured out when leprosy is imposed on his people. Moses was temporarily inflicted (Exodus 4:6-7). Miriam was a leper for seven (7) days because she led a mutiny against Moses (Numbers 12). Naaman was a leper (2 Kings 5), and Jesus encountered other lepers during His ministry.

"AS I SEE IT IN MY MIND," their positioning set up the healing they were about to receive. They saw or heard that Jesus was coming, so they placed themselves where they could be noticed. The ten lepers showed courage and boldness because they knew that this could be their only chance for healing.

Luke 17:13

"They lifted up their voices in one accord, and shouted, Jesus, Master, have mercy on us!" They raised a cry or plea for help, knowing that Jesus had the power to heal them. Now their faith will be exercised because they didn't know how He would heal them, but they believed that He could. *Hebrews 11:1 says, "Now faith is the substance of things hoped for, the evidence of things not seen."*

"AS I SEE IT IN MY MIND," keeping their distance from Jesus, they, hollered, as loud as they could, for Him to have mercy on them because of their suffering due to their leprosy. They collectively put themselves in a position to be seen and heard, not letting this opportunity pass by. Each knew what they had;

each knew what they had to do; each knew what they wanted; and they were together, in unity, as one, suffering from leprosy, wanting Jesus to have mercy on them.

Isn't it ironic how we seemingly get along better when we are suffering from the same or similar ailments, or experiencing the same setbacks? As children of God, we also become unified in a crisis. When situations get tight, we act, hopefully, to make our life and the lives of other's better.

Luke 17:14
"Jesus saw them from afar off, and told them, Go, show yourselves to the priests."

Their courage and hope, their positioning and boldness, and faith has gotten the attention of Jesus. Imagine getting Jesus to see and hear us when family and friends, loved ones, and people in general, can't help us. Notice that Jesus knew exactly what they needed. He then gave them instructions for their healing saying, "*Go; show yourselves to the priests!*"

"Go" is an action verb, meaning we have to do something to activate the blessing, because it becomes null and void if we don't act or move. Also, Jesus knew what the Law of Moses required, that only a priest could declare a leper clean or unclean. Also make note that Jesus healed other lepers and only touched them, so there must be another reason Jesus sent them to see the priests.

"AS I SEE IT IN MY MIND," Jesus knew they had faith, but would they obey Him for their healing? They had to go into the village where they were separated, secluded, and quarantined from everyday life in order to see the priests. And they had pass by some of the congregation, church folk, to get pronounced clean or unclean.

Sometimes we have to go to the very place, or face the same people, who may have been separated from us, for one reason or another, to get our blessing. Jesus wanted to see if they would obey Him, regardless of the risk involved, to be healed. Can't you see them as they started toward the village, that at each step they took, they started feeling stronger and stronger? Yes I believe that as they went, they began to heal, the sores started healing, and their hair started coming back. So each step they took led to their cleansing.

Luke 17:15

The ten lepers hadn't gone very far, didn't even make it to the priests in fact, when one of them stopped and realized that he was totally healed. His flesh had been restored to normal, and instead of him continuing on to see the priests, he decided to go back to the source of his miracle, his blessings, and his healing. He quickly discerned that it was by obeying Jesus, believing that at His command, mercy would descend upon his life. He didn't know what to expect, but stepped toward his healing, by faith, trusting and believing that something was going to happen.

When Jesus tells us to "GO," trust me, good things are going to happen. As he went back, when he saw Jesus, he lifted up his voice loudly, just as he did when he first saw Jesus and asked for mercy, but this time he was praising and glorifying Jesus for the miracle placed on his life. He had a lot to be thankful for, his health restored, his life given back, where he could see and share with family, friends, loved ones, and he could now go to church (synagogue).

Luke 17:16

The man who was once a leper, realized that only God could do this miracle in him, so he wasted no time worshipping God and thanking Jesus for the healing. Never was there a non-Jewish leper healed in the Old Testament, except Naaman, the Syrian. So according to the scriptures, the odds were against a cure of healing pagans who had leprosy. But Jesus made it possible, as through Him all things are possible, for nothing is too hard for God. This leper, one of ten, praised and worshipped the Lord, right then and there. So, I am telling you to give God all the praise and glory while you still have time. We need to practice, make it a habit, to thank God daily for the great blessings He places on our lives.

Lastly, "AS I SEE IT IN MY MIND," Luke leaves the best detail about the man and his actions for the climax of the story. The former leper was a Samaritan, a non-Jew, outside of the Commonwealth of Israel. He was one hated by the Jewish people, a Gentile. Samaritans use a mixture of paganism in their worship of God but look at what happened here. He turned back; he fell at Jesus' feet, worshipped, and gave thanks, praising God. The flow of the verse also implies that the other nine lepers were perhaps Jews, who continued on to see the priests, obeying what Jesus told them to do.

The Samaritan was more grateful than the other nine. When they saw that they had their healing, they were satisfied with it, and kept on walking. But this one leper knew that without Jesus hearing their plea, and acting on his and the others cries for mercy, healing would not have occurred. He was grateful for the change in his life and health and stopped long enough to express his gratitude. I am telling you the truth: gratitude will take you a long way in life.

Luke 17:17

"Jesus asked the Samaritan, 'Were there not ten cleansed, but where are the nine?'"

Jesus knew there were ten of them, who all cried out for mercy, all given the same instructions, all obeyed and received the same healing, but only the Samarian returned to give thanks. The nine seemingly had the attitude that we sometimes have, I'm a child of the King, and I'm doing what Jesus told me to do, so now I can go on with my life forgetting that if it had not been for Jesus, I would not be where I am. Maybe he was more grateful because he knew he was an outsider, compared to the other nine, who were possibly Jews. Or, was it because he recognized he was a new creation? The old man was no more; he was doing acts of worship and praise he had never done before, so he knew a change had come over him. Yes, old things had passed away, and all things had become new. "AS I SEE IT IN MY MIND," God will and still blesses us as individuals, groups, families, and churches, and seeks our worship for all blessings.

Luke 17:18

Jesus asks His third question to the Samaritan, (paraphrased),

"You mean to tell me that I healed all ten of you at the same time and only you, a foreigner, a stranger, a non-Jew, not even of my chosen people, a Gentile, returns to give God glory, no one else, except YOU?" God accepts praise only from a pure heart, and wants us to worship Him in spirit and in truth, and not just for show and tell.

Luke 17:19

Jesus told him to, *"Arise, go your way, your faith has made you well (whole)."*

Jesus tells the man to get up, I've accepted your worship and praise, now it's time to go your way: the way of holy living, the way of helping others, the way of testimony, and live as your healer does, who is Jesus Christ.

"AS I SEE IT IN MY MIND," the Samaritan got much more than the other nine lepers who only got healed (physically), while this man got healing and salvation also. Where do you see salvation in this? Well the word "whole" here means the entire man has been healed, not just the visible or physical part of the man, but the whole man: his spirit has been cleansed also, being changed from unclean to clean. I have no doubt that all ten lepers' flesh was restored like Naaman's, like the flesh of a little child. Only Jesus can make us well, only Jesus can renew us and make us whole. Only Jesus can save us!

Call out to Jesus, tell him what you want, be ready to obey at all costs, sacrificing what you don't want to give, to live. Be thankful in all things, worshipping and praising God right where you are, whether at home, at work, in the streets, at school, wherever you are: *"Behold now is the accepted time: Behold now is the day of salvation."* (2 Corinthians 6:2) (Dakes's Annotated Reference Bible).

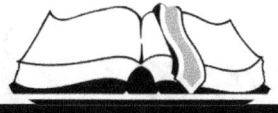

LIFE APPLICATION

Has there been a time when you felt like a leper? If so, describe it. _____
_____
_____
_____
_____

Also, what did Jesus require you to do to change your circumstances?_____
_____
_____

REVIEW / DISCUSSION QUESTIONS

1. What is leprosy? _____
   _____

2. Name two restrictions in life having leprosy created. _____
   _____

3. Was leprosy a "sickness?" _____

4. What made the one leper different from the other nine?
   _____

5. What did you learn from this story? _____
   _____
   _____
   _____

Opening Praise

PSALM 100

"Make a joyful noise unto the Lord, all ye lands. Serve the Lord with gladness; come before his presence with singing. Know ye that the Lord he is God, it is he that hath made us, and not we ourselves; we are his people, and the sheep of his pasture. Enter into his gates with thanks-giving, and into his courts with praise; be thankful unto him, and bless his name. For the Lord is good; his mercy is everlasting; and his truth endureth to all generations."

Lesson No. 3

LEAP OF FAITH: THE WAY WE USE TO HAVE CHURCH

Acts 3:1-11

"Now Peter and John went up together to the temple at the hour of prayer, the ninth hour."

The temple in Jerusalem was situated on a hill, so worshippers had to ascend to God to have church. All of our worship and praise has to go up to God. We lift up holy hands, our prayers and requests go up, and blessings come down from on high. Peter and John were the leaders of the early church, Peter being more vocal, of course. But these two apostles are praying men, prayer partners, on their way to the temple at 3:00 p.m., which is the ninth hour according to the Jewish day, which began at 6:00 a.m. The Jews prayed three times each day: at 9:00 a.m., the third (3rd) hour, at 12 noon, the sixth (6th) hour, and 3:00 p.m., the ninth (9th) hour. Tradition says that these hours were instituted for Abraham, Isaac, and Jacob. The evening devotions included the making of sacrifices and the burning of incense along with prayers. Peter and John set the example for the saints because of the unity between them. They supported and strengthened each other, and they prayed together. As leaders of the church they were to cast the net of the gospel and catch fish (men), and teach them how to be Christians.

A good friend told me that when a baby is born we don't have to teach that child how to do wrong, but we do have to teach the child what is right. Christians are in the same position, we have to be reprogrammed, taught how to live holy, taught how to love our neighbor as ourselves, and taught how to pray.

Acts 3:2

A certain man that was cripple from birth was carried daily, to the Beautiful Gate to beg. I know that I make it sound vague, but that's what happened. Because of his disability, the lame man had to have people's assistance, to aid him, with money, clothes, food and whatever they could give. He was laid at the Beautiful Gate which was a good location because many worshippers and merchants traveled to the temple daily. Worshippers, shoppers, tourists, and people in general would have money to give in tithes and offerings, and buy merchandise while visiting the temple complex. So the chance of the lame man getting alms was very good.

As I said in the lesson about the ten lepers, your positioning determines your blessing. Case in point: if no one had carried this man and laid him at the gate, it is possible he wouldn't have any daily sustenance. But God always places us in strategic positions at the appointed time, so we may be blessed. There is no telling how many years he had been doing his daily ritual (I say years, because he was a grown man.) So I say, never give up, struggle to survive if you have to, because trouble don't last always!

Acts 3:3

There isn't any indication that this man knew who Peter and John were, but "AS I SEE IT IN MY MIND," the man wasn't deaf, and he wasn't blind. I read that scripture says he was there daily, and I see Peter and John going to the temple daily. So I really believe that he had possibly seen them before, but may have never had a chance to ask them for alms. Or, he had heard of the many signs and wonders done by the apostles that are not even written in this book. So when he saw his opportunity, he did what he was accustomed to do; he asked for alms. I caution each of you to be careful when people are asking for food, rides home, or money, because we who are not in their shoes, judge before we act. Whether we give or not, we judge, but be thankful it's not you, especially in these times.

Acts 3:4

Peter deserves a lot of credit because he could have ignored him, like we do sometimes, or he could have told the man to leave them alone.

Hebrews 13:1-2

"Let brotherly love continue. Be not forgetful to entertain strangers: for thereby some have entertained angels unawares."

AS I SEE IT IN MY MIND," Peter fastening, (looking steadily, staring), at him, was spiritually discerning what the man really needed. Was it food, money, clothes, or was it something more? Peter along with John, said, *"Look on us!"* Peter is using the power of the Holy Spirit to see the man's needs, and the power to heal him, both physically and spiritually. When God heals, he heals the body and the spirit, He makes us new. *"Therefore if any man be in Christ, he is a new creature, or creation, old things are passed away, behold, all things are become new"* (2 Corinthians 5:17, Dakes's Annotated Reference Bible). Peter wanted the man's undivided attention, what God wants from us, but seldom gets. Peter was about to change this man's life, so he wanted him to understand what he was giving him, an alms, an envelope with healing inside, a gift from God.

Acts 3:5

The man gave heed preparing himself to receive what Peter was about to give him. When we expect a gift or a blessing, we pay attention. This is a bold statement: people in need should always expect to receive a blessing from God's people. That's why He blesses us, so we can bless someone else.

Acts 3:6

Peter let the lame man know that they were in the same situation, they were both broke, but Peter told the man that I do have something that is more valuable than silver and gold. I have the power of the Holy Spirit upon me, and "I*n the name of Jesus, rise up and walk!*" WHAT!!!

"AS I SEE IT IN MY MIND," the lame man had to be thinking, you are telling me to rise up and walk! Do you realize that I've been crippled since birth? Do you know that I've never walked in my life? Let me explain my life: people have been laying me here for years; I can't even get myself up, and you say you are giving me something?

The apostles possessed the power of healing given to them by Jesus (Matthew 10:1). Now Peter exhibits the Christian's *"Power of Attorney"* (John 16:23). All of us who are in Christ have this power, and it puzzles me why we don't use the gifts that we have. Peter also asks the man to show some faith. Likewise, all you have to do is believe that it is possible, because through God all things are possible!

Acts 3:7

Peter knew the man was lame, had never walked, and to rise up would be impossible for him. So Peter reached down and took the man by his right hand, and lifted him up. We, today should follow Peter's example by getting down on a needy person's level. If someone is down in the ditch, get down there with them, and lift them up. We should always be willing to lift up each other spiritually, or say a kind word or even know that a smile can lift up a bowed down head.

I have an inspiring scripture that I recite to lift up myself and others when feeling down and out. According to the Word in Psalm 24:7-10 (part B) *"Lift up ye heads, O ye gates; and be ye lift up, ye everlasting doors; and the King of glory shall come in. Who is this King of glory? The Lord strong and mighty, the Lord mighty in battle. Lift up your heads, O ye gates; and the King of glory shall come in. Who is this King of glory? The Lord of hosts, He is the King of glory. Selah."* (Dakes's Annotated Reference Bible)

As soon as the lame man stood up, the Word says, "Immediately, his feet and ankle bones received strength." When God heals, it is at once, instantly, no check-ups, no physical therapy is needed. When God heals it is a complete healing. I will revisit complete healing later. From my personal experience, I have suffered sprains and broken ankles many times during my basketball playing days. I also had my knee scoped, and on every occasion I could barely stand, much less walk, without crutches or a cane.

Acts 3:8

What happened here? First, he leaped up! This in itself is a miracle. Imagine, never walking, and suddenly you have strength in your feet and ankles, and legs to be able to leap. He took, "A LEAP OF FAITH!" The lame man knew he didn't have anything to lose, but everything to gain. After leaping, he stood, again he "immediately," had enough strength in his lower body, which previously was impotent, to support the weight of his upper body. Amazing! He was able to leap, stood on his own, and kept his balance, a miracle in my mind, but I do see things differently than others.

Next, he walked - indeed another miracle!!! Even babies must learn to crawl first, then pull themselves up, learn to maintain their balance, and fall several times before they are able to walk. God's healing is complete, without flaws, and the whole man was healed. WHY? I'm running the light here, I do that once in a while. Because he didn't just walk around, or go home, he started walking to church with the apostles. He now had a mind to fellowship with the saints. His healing gave him the desire to praise God, and he had good reason to jump up and shout because he was healed. He didn't even tell people he was healed, for all could see the miracle that had occurred in his life.

Now all of us are supposed to have a praise in our mouths at all times. But we walk in church networking, as we call it now. Really, it's running our mouths in one way, or another. But as this man walked in. He was leaping when he hit the door, no music yet, no prayers yet, no songs by the choir to make him leap up, he was stirred up by the fact he had been healed. Next, he was praising God. He didn't come like a lot of us do, speaking to folks, discussing current events, gossiping, doing business deals, etc. He entered the temple walking, leaping, and praising God, the way we should all enter. He didn't need motivating, he was healed, he had his blessing, and he was full of joy and thanksgiving, and couldn't hold his peace. God not only heals the physical deformities in us, but He specializes in creating a spiritual awakening in us, that gives us a heart of thanksgiving and worship.

Acts 3:9

Everybody saw the man as he was now walking, openly acknowledging that God had healed him through His servants Peter and John. He wasn't putting on a show, but his actions proved the miraculous healing, and his spirit validated that he was a new man.

"AS I SEE IT IN MY MIND," before his healing, when he was laying at the gate, he exhibited no inkling of worship or praise. All he did was beg all day, and he seemingly had no joy, nothing to live for, nothing to look forward to, except an alms, the same old daily routine. But now, after Peter and John performed a miracle in him, his focus and attitude changed. He isn't dependent on others anymore. He's not begging. His mind and spirit has new meaning. He has a testimony to tell others of his healing, and now he has a new life to live. When God heals us, He takes whatever sin(s) that are crippling us, lifts us up out of the miry clay, and makes us complete. Then we should rejoice and worship God in spirit and in truth.

Acts 3:10

Whenever a miracle occurs, it has an effect on the one receiving it and the ones who witness or see the results of it. Miracles are supernatural events that only God can enact, or one of His representative. In this case Peter and John were endowed with miracle working power. The people who saw the man knew it was him, recognizing he was the lame man who laid at the temple gate daily and begged.

An authentic miracle is one that is evident to everyone, no illusion, no TV, no cameras, nothing is hidden, and every miracle performed by Moses or one of God's prophets, by Jesus, and by the Apostles, were done openly, not secretly or behind closed doors.

This supernatural act of God had the people stirred up, they were wondering, and amazed about what had happened to this man. People always try to figure out how or why certain things happen. They are surprised at miracles which occur in this day and time. I don't believe in coincidences. I know that God is in control at all times, no matter who thinks they are driving! Nothing happens unless God wills it, and gives His approval.

Miracles in people serve as "change agents," making us what God wants us to be, for His glory. Lastly, the lame man never said thank you to the apostles, because he knew a higher power had touched him. He recognized that he had been, "Blessed by the Best!"

Acts 3:11

The lame man held onto Peter and John, the avenue which God used to heal him. This man's life had been turned around physically, he gained independence, his social and economic status was changed, and spiritually he was a new creation in Christ.

Do you remember where you were, what you were, and where you were going before He lifted you up and healed you of the sins that so easily beset you? We need to hold onto God's unchanging hand at all times, because all our blessings come from above. The people were so excited they ran together to Peter, John, and the now healed man, still wondering what all had happened. This reminds me of things people do when they get excited: they run and celebrate, similar to mobs running onto a ball field when their team wins a championship.

Was it Peter and John who healed him, or was it God? "AS I SEE IT IN MY MIND," man works no miracles, only God working through man can miracles be performed.

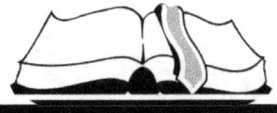

LIFE APPLICATION

This story should have inspired strength, courage, hope, faith in God, or faith in the supernatural power of God. Take one of these, and write about the one that touched you the most. Please write from your heart and use another sheet of paper, if necessary.

_____
_____
_____
_____
_____
_____
_____
_____
_____
_____
_____
_____
_____

REVIEW / DISCUSSION QUESTIONS

1. Where was the Beautiful Gate?_____
   _____

2. Why was this man lying at the Beautiful Gate?_____
   _____

3. When Peter and John could not give money, what did they give?_____

4. What caused this man to leap with joy?_____
   _____

Opening Praise

PSALM 107:1-7

"Oh, give thanks to the Lord, for he is good! For his mercy endures forever. Let the redeemed of the Lord say so, Whom He has redeemed from the hand of the enemy. And gathered out of the lands, from the east and from the west. From the north and the south. They wandered in the wilderness in a desolate way; they found no city to dwell in. Hungry and thirsty, their souls fainted in them. Then they cried out to the Lord in their trouble. And He delivered them out of their distress. And he led them forth by the right way. That they might go to a city for a dwelling place."

Lesson No. 4 — HOW TO GET PRAYERS ANSWERED

II Chronicles 7:14

"If my people, which are called by my name, shall humble themselves, and pray, and seek my face, and turn from their wicked ways; then will I hear from heaven, and will forgive their sin, and will heal their land." (Dakes's Annotated Reference Bible)

I believe this scripture sets forth a pattern for prayer that if used will bring about great intervention from the Lord. Let's take a look at it point by point.

IF MY PEOPLE - ("If" - on condition that; whether or not; an assumption or condition" (Webster's Dictionary). God is telling Israel, and us today, that if you do (keep) my Word, I will do (keep) my promises. Israel in that day, and Christians today have a record, the Bible, that we read demonstrates how God has kept every promise He has ever made. But God, "AS I SEE IT IN MY MIND," gives us a choice, as the car commercial says, "You can go with this, or you can go with that." You have a choice to live as God would have you live or not. This is described as freewill.

2 Peter 3:9 says, *"The Lord is not slack concerning His promise, as some men count slackness; but is long-suffering to us-ward, not willing that any should perish, but that all should come to repentance."* (Dakes's Annotated Reference Bible)

WHICH ARE CALLED BY MY NAME - Numbers 6:27 says, *"So they (Aaron and his sons) shall put my name on the children of Israel, and I will bless them."* Deuteronomy 28:10 says, *"That all the peoples of the earth shall see that you are called by the name of the Lord, and they shall be afraid of you."*

When the text was recorded, only Israel was designated as God's chosen people. Now in our time, Christians are God's people also. There are four conditions that Israel, in biblical times, and we today must meet. They are:

1. **Humble themselves** — Be not high-minded, too proud, not thinking of yourself better than others, remembering who you were, and who you are now in Christ. [Humility]

2. **And pray** — Man ought to always pray, thanking God for all blessings, and pray without ceasing. Jesus prayed constantly, and He had the full measure of the Spirit. Confess your faults one to another, and pray one for another, that ye may be healed. The effectual

fervent prayer of a righteous man availeth much. Pray for needs, not wants. Thank God for all blessings.

3. **And seek my face** — Look to God for guidance and direction. We should ask for His advice in all aspects of life. This is a flaw that I and a lot of Christians have. I, we, don't seek God in every area of our lives. We make split decisions without seeking guidance and direction from God.

4. **And turn from their wicked ways** — Repentance is required for forgiveness of all sins. 1st John 1:8-10 says, *"If we say that we have no sin, we deceive ourselves, and the truth is not in us. If we confess our sins, he is faithful and just to forgive us our sins, and to cleanse us from all unrighteousness. If we say that we have not sinned, we make him a liar, and his word is not in us."* (Dakes's Annotated Reference Bible)

Romans 3:23
"For all have sinned, and come short of the glory of God". (Dakes's Annotated Reference Bible)

What is wickedness? "AS I SEE IT IN MY MIND," the term describes practicing evil, thinking bad things to do or say, unholy living. My mind recalls an Old Testament verse that illustrates my thoughts because sometimes, as Christians, we do what is right in our own minds.

Judges 21:25
"In those days there was no king in Israel: every man did that which was right in his own eyes". So let's be clear: if what you are

thinking or doing is not of God, its wickedness. 1 Corinthians 10:31 reads, *"Whether therefore ye eat, or drink, or whosoever ye do, do all to the glory of God."* (Dakes's Annotated Reference Bible)

We find three BLESSINGS FOR ISRAEL (AND US), listed "if" conditions are met, or "if" we are obedient. These three blessings outline what God will do in response to prayer that is acceptable unto Him.

1. **Then will I hear from heaven** — 2 Chronicles 6:26, 27, and 30, *"When the heaven is shut- up, and there is no rain, because they have sinned against thee; yet if they pray toward this place, and confess thy name, and turn from their sin, when thou dost afflict them; Then hear thou from heaven, and forgive the sins of thy servants, and of thy people Israel, when thou has taught them the good way, wherein they should walk; and send rain upon thy land, which thou hast given unto thy people for an inheritance. Then hear thou from heaven thy dwelling place, and forgive, and render unto every man according unto all his ways, whose heart thou knowest; (for thou only knowest the hearts of the children of men."*

Between the Old and New Testaments some 400 years went by when heaven was shut- up for prayers from God's people because of their sins. God heard their petitions, their cries, their pleas for mercy, but He didn't answer, or did He? No, is also an answer. God, foreknew that He was going to send His Son Jesus.

2. **I will forgive their sin** — Only God can forgive sin, but confession is necessary first, then repentance is

required of Israel and us to be blessed. God has been forgiving men of sin since sin came into the world - Genesis 3.

3. **I will heal their land** — Israel, like us has not met the four conditions. Therefore, the blessings were never realized in its completion. God will always keep His promises; it is up to us to uphold our part by obeying his Word.

"AS I SEE IT IN MY MIND," God's conditions must be met, and we must fulfill the requirements God mandates to be blessed and our prayers heard. We always get an answer from God; it may not be the answer you want, but it's the answer you need. Why is our world and the world at large like it is? Read the verse again, God has promised to bless His people, but don't linger, don't hesitate, we have not kept our part of the agreement.

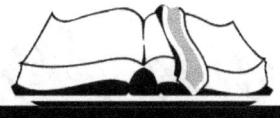

LIFE APPLICATION

Name three reasons why this scripture is important to every Believer.

1. _____
2. _____
3. _____

Take time to Memorize 2 Chronicles 7:14 today. Write it out here by memory once and you have memorized it.

_____
_____

REVIEW / DISCUSSION QUESTIONS

1. What important Christian benefit does this scripture focus upon? _____

2. This is classified as a "conditional" verse. Explain what that means. _____
   _____

3. Identify the two parts to this scripture and to whom they apply to. _____
   _____

4. How can this scripture help you in your own personal prayer life? _____
   _____

Opening Praise
JOHN 15:15-17

"No longer do I call you servants, for a servant does not know what his master is doing; but I have called you friends, for all things that I heard from My Father I have made known to you. You did not chose me, but I chose you and appointed you that you should go forth and bear fruit, and that your fruit should remain, that whatever you ask the Father in my name He may give you. These things I command you, that you love one another."

Lesson No. 5 — WHO WE ARE IN CHRIST

1st Peter 2:9-10

"But ye are a chosen generation, a royal priesthood, a holy nation, a peculiar people, that ye should shew forth the praises of Him who hath called you out of darkness into His marvelous light; which in time past were not a people, but now are the people of God, which had not obtained mercy, but now have obtained mercy." (Dakes's Annotated Reference Bible)

But ye are - Peter is writing to Christians, believers, and saved people. What are believers to God? We find the answer to this question in 1st Peter 2:5: *"Ye also, as lively stones, are built up a spiritual house, a holy priesthood, to offer up spiritual sacrifices, acceptable to God by Jesus Christ"*. Also Titus 2:14 adds to this by saying, *"Who gave Himself for us, that He may redeem us from all iniquity, and purify unto Himself a peculiar people, zealous of good works."* (Dakes's Annotated Reference Bible)

"AS I SEE IT IN MY MIND," we who in times past were sinners, and now we who are the redeemed, are because of

Christ. (We are saints who have the capacity to commit sins, but saved by the shed blood of Jesus Christ). We should live as spiritual temples, holy before God and man, always praising God for redeeming us. The Bible teaches that we should do well unto all mankind but especially to those who are of the household of faith. What they, and (we) were is past, what they, and (we) are now is present. They nor we today, are strangers anymore, but now we are accepted as joint-heirs with Christ.

A chosen generation — Chosen - to select, to prefer as an option, elite. (Webster's Dictionary) Deuteronomy 7:6, 8 records, *"For you are a holy people to the Lord your God; the Lord your God has chosen you to be a people for Himself, a special treasure above all the peoples on the face of the earth. The Lord did not set His love on you nor choose you because you were more in number than any other people, for you were the least of all peoples; but because the Lord loves you, and because He would keep the oath which He swore to your fathers, the Lord has brought you out with a mighty hand, and redeemed you from the house of bondage, from the hand of Pharaoh king of Egypt."*

Also Deut. 14:2 adds, *"For you are a holy people to the Lord your God, and the Lord has chosen you to be a people unto Himself, a special treasure above all the peoples who are on the face of the earth"* (Dake's Annotated Reference Bible.)

We have been selected, by God's choices. We were preferred over another as an option, God's own people, the Jews rejected Him, and so salvation was given to us, Gentiles, although we don't deserve it. "AS I SEE IT IN MY MIND," we are the elite ones chosen because of the promise God made to the fathers, but also we are special, the top of the class, the cream of the crop, the best, not because of our goodness, but because of Christ.

A royal priesthood — We are royal - relating to kings and queens. Now we are royal (a higher status), because Jesus is our King, who is now in glory. We are priests, able to offer up praises, prayers, and sacrifices to God, meaning we have access to God ourselves, not only through the man of God. Exodus 19:6 – "*And ye shall be unto me a kingdom of priests, and a holy nation. These are the words which thou shalt speak unto the children of Israel*" (Dakes's Annotated Reference Bible). We are in a unique relationship with God, priests, servants of God and His church. A holy nation - set apart, separated, sanctified, we are sacred, meaning we are dedicated to worship.

"AS I SEE IT IN MY MIND," this is saying that we should be striving to give God as much time as we do our hobbies, our vocations, and our passions. Our lives, each day, should be lived for Christ, spending more of our energies doing good, helping our neighbors, and walking in the light, setting good examples for the world to see and emulate. We can all do better and improve some areas in our lives. All of us as Christians are now one nation, regardless of individual race, color, or creed. We are one, under one head (God), and touch and agree on the same principles, and are saved by the precious blood of Christ.

A peculiar people — Peculiar here doesn't mean strange or odd, although I will admit God's people are some weird folks, including myself, sometimes. We get emotional when others don't cry, shout, and get happy. Those around us may not understand our actions. People thought Jesus was strange, different, and He was. But the word peculiar means purchased, brought, redeemed. How? By the precious blood of Christ, who died in our place so that we can show forth the praises of Him who hath called you out of darkness into his marvelous light. This means we should show the evidence of Christian virtues in our lives, such as, wisdom, knowledge justice, truth, grace, peace, joy, love, faith and holiness. As the old folks would say, if you are saved you ought to show some signs, some evidence that you are in Christ, and Christ is in you, by the way you walk, talk, and how you live. God gets glory and praise when we represent him properly. Simply put, your actions speak louder than your words.

Who hath called you out of darkness - To call out to someone, to deliver, save, and rescue. God has been calling out to His people for generations. He has sent to man carriers of the Word, prophet after prophet, but finally He sent His only begotten Son, Jesus Christ, to not only show us the pathway of righteousness, but to teach us how we should live and treat others. Darkness represent sin, and God has, "AS I SEE IT IN MY MIND," summoned us (called) us to no longer live as sinners.

Into His marvelous light - God has not only taken us from being in the dark, or unable to see our way. Why? Because sin distorts our vision, sometimes blinding us. But God has given us knowledge and truth through His Word, and salvation through His Son Jesus, who is the light of the world. "AS I SEE IT IN MY MIND," Jesus taught us, died for us, and nowadays we have no excuse for our ignorance or our sins which we commit sometimes (every now and then). We have the record, we have the promises of God, contained in the Bible, His Holy Word. Jesus said, *"As long as I am in the world, I am the light of the world"* John 9:5 (Dakes's Annotated Reference Bible). Which in time past, were not a people, but now are the people of God.

Hosea 1:10 says, *"Yet the number of the children of Israel shall be as the sand of the sea, which cannot be measured or numbered; and it shall come to pass, in the place where it was said unto them, ye are not my people, there it shall be said unto them. Ye are the sons of the living God." Again* Hosea in 2:23 says, *"And I will sow her unto me in the earth; and I will have mercy upon her that had not obtained mercy, and I will say to them which were not my people, Thou art my people, and they shall say, Thou art my God."* (Dakes's Annotated Reference Bible)

According to Romans 9:24-26, *"Even us, whom He hath called, not of the Jews only, but also of the Gentiles? As he saith also in Hosea, I will call them my people, and her beloved, which was not beloved. And it shall come to pass, that in the place where it was said unto them. Ye are not my people, there shall be called the children of the living God"* (Dakes's Annotated Reference Bible).

"AS I SEE IT IN MY MIND," I as a black man, can identify with this verse, from a human point of view, but the verse is deeper than being about a black man, or any other man from any country. What God is telling us is that now you are a child of God! You have been chosen above all the people in the world, and now you are God's chosen people, which had not obtained mercy, but now have obtained mercy. But what is mercy? Mercy is an act of forgiveness and compassion. It is sympathy for someone who is suffering or distressed. We didn't deserve God feeling sorry for us, nor do we warrant forgiveness, because we have sinned against God, and haven't kept His commandments. The devil or this world doesn't care if we sin or break the laws of the land, or God's laws. While we were yet sinners, Christ died for us.

BUT NOW:

Ephesians 2:12-13 — *"That in that time ye were without Christ, being aliens from the commonwealth of Israel, and strangers from the covenants of promise, having no hope, and without God in the world."* (Dakes's Annotated Reference Bible).

BUT NOW in Christ Jesus ye who sometimes were far off are made nigh by the blood of Christ. Ephesian 5:8, *"For ye were sometimes darkness,*

BUT NOW *are ye light in the Lord, walk as children of light"* (Dakes's Annotated Reference Bible).

"**BUT NOW** *ye also put off all these, anger, wrath, malice, blasphemy, filthy communication out of your mouth. Lie not one to another, seeing that ye have put off the old man with his deeds. And have put on the new man, which is renewed in knowledge after the image of Him that created him"* (Colossians 3:8-10 Dakes's Annotated Reference Bible).

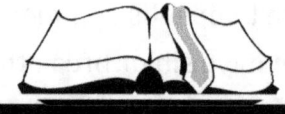

LIFE APPLICATION

Explain how this lesson has given you a clearer understanding of who you are in Christ.

_____
_____
_____
_____
_____

REVIEW / DISCUSSION QUESTIONS

1. What primary subject does this lesson cover?

2. How important is it to you to know who you are in Christ?

3. Name two key aspects discussed about you as a child of God?

4. Name one person you will share this lesson with and why you think it will help them.

Now unto Him who is able to keep you
From falling, and to present you faultless
Before His presence
Of this glory with exceeding joy,
To the only wise God our Savior,
Be glory and majesty,
Dominion and power,
Both now and ever.
Jude 1:24
AMEN.
The End.

Reference Resources

Some scripture references and quotes were taken from these resources:

Dake, J.F. (1963). Dakes's Annotated Reference Bible (Old and New Testaments). Dake Bible Sales, Inc. Lawrenceville, Georgia

Dorsey, T.A. The Old Ship of Zion; R.H. Publishing, Nashville, Tennessee

Holman Christian Standard Bible. (2010) Holman Bible Publishers, Nashville, Tennessee

MacArthur, J. (1997). The MacArthur Study Bible. Thomas Nelson, Inc.

Mandino, O. (1975). The God Memorandum. Frederick Fell Publishers, Inc. Hollywood, Florida

Matthew, H., Matthew Henry's Commentary on the Whole Bible.

Merriam-Webster., Webster's Dictionary

The Holy Bible, King James Version

The New King James Study Bible

The NIV Bible

About the Author

The Author was born the eldest son of Reuben C. Lawrence, Sr. and Betty J. Hughley Lawrence on May 10, 1954, in Chattanooga, Tennessee. The majority of Lawrence's growth and development was on Lookout Mountain, Tennessee, where his parents resided in the very house my father was raised in. He was educated at an early age at Lookout Mountain Colored School where all black students were called "Negroes" at the time. In 1962 the Hamilton County Board of Education opened its doors to Blacks, due to desegregation, where the law mandated that Black and White students had to attend school together. Mr. Lawrence had the honor of being one of the first Blacks to attend Lookout Mountain Elementary School.

Reuben's parents were, and my Father still is, a hard-working middle class citizen, who believed in God, the church, education, working hard, and making an honest living. On June 11, 2013, his precious mother transitioned to heaven.

He graduated from Howard High School in 1972, and attended college for a while. Reuben met his high school sweetheart in 1970, while in the 10th grade, and married DeBarbara Toney on December 22, 1973. God blessed their union with 35 years of marriage, two children, and four grand-children. His dear wife, DeBarbara departed this life on December 20, 2008 and now resides in heaven with Jesus.

Lawrence accepted Christ at an early age and was baptized at his home church, First Baptist Church of Lookout Mountain,

Tennessee, which was established in 1904. The current edifice was built in 1955. Lawrence has served in many positions in the church, including Trustee, Sunday school teacher, and was ordained as a Deacon in 1982. Mr. Lawrence is extremely proud to say that his entire immediate family are Christians. He is currently, a member of Mt. Canaan Baptist Church located in Chattanooga, Tennessee, serving its Senior Pastor, Dr. Ternae Jordan.